Marci Nelligan

The Ghost Manada

© 2016 Marci Nelligan

ISBN: 978-0-9979524-0-7

1. American poetry—21st century. 2. Poets, American—21st Century.

Black Radish Books

www.blackradishbooks.com

First printing 2016 in the United States of America

Cover art: Untitled, Anthony Ryan, 2016.
Images accompanying the text: Untitled, Anthony Ryan, 2016.

Book design and layout: Black Radish Books

All rights reserved. No part of this book may be reproduced, stored in a retrieval system, or transmitted by any means, electronic, mechanical, photocopying, recording, or otherwise, without prior permission of the publisher.

Distributed by:
Small Press Distribution
1341 Seventh Street
Berkeley, CA 94710-1409
spd@spdbooks.org

I would like to acknowledge some of the female poets I am indebted to— who have infiltrated the page, who have thrown wide the doors despite the silence & obstacle imposed upon them. I offer their names against the erasure of the female, which is everywhere, and notably in the novel this project engages with.

Gertrude Stein; Gwendolyn Brooks; Audre Lorde, Juliana Spahr; Alice Notley; Amy King; Susana Gardner; Nicole Mauro; Marthe Reed; Carrie Hunter; Wanda Colemen; Robin Coste Lewis; Tonya Foster; Patricia Lockwood; Emily Dickinson; Cole Swensen, HD, Bernadette Mayer; Leslie Scalapino; Meg Day; Brenda Shaughnessy; Louise Glück; Ansel Elkins; Pattie McCarthy; Yona Harvey; Tameka Cage Conley; Jena Osman; Katie Ford; Jen Hofer; Dolores Dorantes; Joanne Kyger; Shelia Murphy; Joan Rettalack; Marjorie Perloff; Fanny Howe; Susan Howe; Eileen Myles; Maggie Nelson; PJ Harvey; Patti Smith; Elizabeth Willis; Dorothea Lasky; Nada Gordon; Elizabeth Bryant; Jill Stengel; Mackenzie Carignan; Harryette Mullen; Dawn Lundy Martin; Hoa Nguyen; Judith Johnson; Lorine Niedecker; Rae Armantrout; Dodie Bellamy; Mei-mei Berssenbrugge; Erin Moure; Lee Ann Brown; Dodie Bellamy; Rosemary Waldrop; Maxine Chernoff; Carolyn Forché; Johanna Drucker; Rachel Blau DuPlessis; Katheleen Fraser; Barbara Guest; Lyn Hejinian; Myung Mi Kim; Theresa Cha; Jennifer Moxley; Joan Retallack; Anne Tardos; Anne Carson; Cecilia Vicuña; Marjorie Welish; Hannah Weiner; Mary Ruefle; Denise Levertov; Denise Dhomhnaill; Matthea Harvey; Jennifer Knox; Shanna Compton; Mary Szybist; Anna Akhmatova; Wislava Szymborska; Marianne Moore; Chana Bloch; Bhanu Kapil Ryder; Anne Waldman; Alejandra Pizarnik; Adrienne Rich; Jayne Cortez; Carolyn Rodgers; Elizabeth Bishop; Maxine Kumin; Michelle Detorie; Rachel Shukert; Reb Livingston; Lydia Davis; Emily Brönte; Jessica Smith; Pattie McCarthy; Karen Randall; Paige Taggart; Daina Savage; Lori Anderson Moseman; Judy Halebsky; Thea Hillman; Chana Kronfeld; Cara Benson; Oni Buchanan; Erin Dorney; Barbara Strasko; Brenda Iijima; Jena Osman; Dawn Lonsinger; Erin Belleu; Cate Marvin; CD Wright; Dana Levin; Danielle Pafunda; Brenda Hillman; Toi Derricott; Meena Alexander; TJ Jarrett; Rita Dove; Claudia Rankine; Dorianne Laux; Heather McHugh; Mary Jo Bang; Camille Rankine; Carrie Hunter; Ethel Rackin; Hassen Saker; K. Lorraine Graham; Sharon Mesmer; Elizabeth Workman; Juliana Leslie; Elizabeth Treadwell; Emily Critchley; Megan Kaminski; Kaia Sand; Megan Burns; Eileen Tabios; Sarah Anne Cox; Susan Schultz; Catherine Daly; Danielle Vogel; Kristen Prevallet; Lisa Robertson; Jen Tynes; Deborah Poe; Jen Scappettone; Noelle Kocot; Daisy Fried; Gwyn McVay; Ginger Ko; Jennifer Tamayo; Nikki Wallschlaeger; Wanda Phipps; Erica Hunt; Julia Bloch; Yedda Morrison; Rebecca Wolff; Sawako Nakayasu; Anne Gorrick; Dana Teen Lomax; Norma Cole; Laura Moriarty; Diane DiPrima; Megan Burns; Amy Lowell; Sylvia Plath; Margaret Atwood; Carrie Pickett; Sappho; Tracy K. Smith; Kathy Acker; Helen Adam; Elizabeth Alexander; Anne Boyer; Nicole Brossard; Laynie Browne; Tina Darragh; La Tasha N. Nevada Diggs; Linh Dinh; kari edwards; Susan Gevirtz; Ange Mlinko; Carol Mirakove; Jenn McCreary; Mina Loy; Ann Lauterbach; Myung Mi Kim; Elizabeth Bishop; Edna St. Vincent Millay; Erica Kaufman; June Jordan; Lisa Jarnot; Carla Harryman; Maya Angelou; Jorie Graham; Renée Gladman; Lisa Robinson; Evie Shockley; Mónica de la Torre; Stephanie Young; Nikki Giovanni; Lucile Clifton; Dorthea Tanning; Judy Grahn; Alice Fulton; Muriel Rukeyser; Sonia Sanchez; May Swenson; Karen Weiser; U.A. Fanthorpe; Edith Södergran; Nelly Sachs; Gloria Fuertes.

Table of Contents

Introduction vi
Ghosts at the Threshold 1
Ghost Lyrics 1 11
The First Violence 31
The Meridians 37
Ghost Lyrics 2 41
The Second Violence 59
Ghost Lyrics 3 65
This Final Margin 81

This book is the result of a long occupation with Cormac McCarthy's novel, *Blood Meridian*, which enticed and held me with its rich, archaic language and its unforgiving darkness. I was caught in the tension between the human capacity for ugliness, and our simultaneous stretch toward beauty. That the astonishing violence and genocide depicted in *Blood Meridian* are largely taken from life should not shock me, but continues to, despite the mirror it holds up to the present. I wanted to give myself the reins McCarthy takes—to write in the freedom of ancient, sound-driven language—to follow the lyric's pulse—while going deeply into the place of violence, death, human capacity, and American mythology. In addition, I wanted to speak my outrage and confusion over the nearly complete omission of women from the book, a source of despair and argument for me, an internal conflict at being so drawn to what actively excludes.

And so the sections of this book reflect those influences: "Ghost Lyrics" are inspired by language and sound; "The Violences" assault the structure and solidity of the poems on the page; "The Meridians" are an interlude of navigation and placement; the opening and closing sections take on the role of women in the novel. My great thanks to Cormac McCarthy for this and all of his writing. Huge gratitude to my dear pal Anthony Ryan, for collaborating on this and many other 'projects' throughout our long friendship. My greatest thanks to Lee, Sonya, and Dahlia, to whom this book, and all the rest of me, belongs.

And thank you to the editors of *Fledgling Rag* and *Dusie*, who published early excerpts of this work.

"It is a violence within that protects us from a violence without." –*Wallace Stevens*

"The other side of the mind is now exposed—the dark side that comes uppermost in solitude, not the light side that shows in company." –*Virginia Woolf*

"The ugly fact is books are made out of books. The novel depends for its life on the novels that have been written." –*Cormac McCarthy*

Ghosts at the Threshold

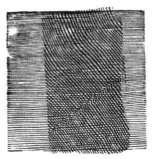

> A wo   man
> appea   red in
> the   door-
> way   of the
> house   and
> one   of the
> Mex-   icans
> spoke   to her
> and she went
> in   again.

In this novel of nomadic slaughter—in the canyon between language's beauty and man's ugliness— there are hardly any female characters. Many are pictured in doorways, a curious but persistent fact. Here, the excerpts in which they appear, but altered—the poem a door, a letting out and letting in.

She h	ad come to
the d	oor. She
stood	in the hallw
ay ho	lding the
cand	le and brush-
ing h	er hair back
with	one hand and
she	watched him
desc	end into the
dark	of the stair-
well	and then she
pull	ed the door
shut	behind her.

The door as sudden shut, and I, I lost, was passing by—lost doubly, but by contrast most, enlightening misery.—Emily Dickinson

A door slammed. An
old   woman came
do   wn the lane
past   the daubed sty
wal   ls through the
mist   carrying a yoke
of j   ars.

A door's liminal hinge/entrance exit, route or bar.
Determined by who builds. One reason why the witches
salt their thresholds.

The	woman
ope	ned the
doo	r and
loo	ked at
him	

Her crouch at the margin, which is also a door. A bell, a bell. A warning bell.

The	woman
app	eared
at t	he door
aga	in.

When something is insistently absent it is everywhere there. And what you cannot see just might. Might be the thing that makes you.

And the
youn g girls
of th e city
were board-
ed up and
seen no
more.

No women guard these openings; such as gates need keeping, these unkept. Knock, keep knocking. The soul selects her own then shuts. Then shuts the door.

The old	lady had
come to	the back
door a w	oman
speaking	in
Spanish	

The point of placing a woman in this way. To emphasize her hostage. Or heighten her remove. The door a spell. The spell her hand might make.

In a	door
way	a young
girl	whose
bea	uty be
com	es the
flo	wers ab
out.	

Make the chaos on one side obey the rigors of the other.
Then close the valves of her attention.

A woman in a silk kimono
ope   ned the
do   or and
loo   ked out at
him.   Behind her
in t   he room a
can   dle burned
at t   he table
wh   en the
wo   man asked
him   what he
wan   ted he
turn   ed without
speak   ing

I stuff the pages bit by bit between my legs and call it women's literature; write a lock & twist in it a key.

Ghost Lyrics 1

The italicized text at the top of each page is taken from Blood Meridian *and inspired the composition of each respective poem.*

All night the wind blew and the fine dust set their teeth on edge. Sand in everything, grit in all they ate.

Summer and everything has burned
into the brown neglect of autumn—
the moon lisping in the sky
like antic death's new suit.

This desert, our present
a long, flat palm examined
by the sun, a fateful eustacy
whose black wings signal
feast or fest
food or feed.

Eternity insists the sand
admit the fine ash
of your body, erodes the letters
of your windblown name.
Elsewhere, the skirmish
has new blades, and who are we
to punish and what are we to be?

I suckle the rock's red veins—
bleed out, bleed days,
while at the withered spoon of once
what I took for hope was weather
what I thought the sky,
decay.

The wind ever-blows
the land into the sea—
the gritty, nameless sea
whose salt is not the body
but the remnant of the body,
whose susurrus the moan
of all we used to be.

The judge raised the parasol and adjusted his parcels. Perhaps, he called, perhaps you have seen this place in a dream.

I was saying something—

> was born and then
> > a body came to claim
> > & the body is my question, not ante-/post-
>
> but now.

I dreamed this before

> and here was another—
>
> > woman, man & what
> > we've made.
> > The consequence
> > the body brings—
> > no matter I own it;
> > no matter not.

I was saying something—

> making words from simple sound
> or catching life
> in its thin tissue.

Was speaking when—

Was born and then—

and then.

Before man was, war waited for him. The ultimate trade awaiting its ultimate practitioner. That is the way it was and will be. That way and not some other way.

Something fits
into this emptiness
the way words
conjugate our mouths.

There was darkness
at the center so we filled
it in with god—
saints to walk
the earth with their eyes
in their hands bleeding
out fresh metaphors.

Hole, dark hole—
something spells there
foulbreathed & beautiful.
Pulls us ever in.

What use the spear
but the wound—
the void's great
capability.
What sentence
in the sequence
of our names.

The riders squatted at the fires and boiled water and drank coffee and roasted meat and lay down to sleep among the dead.

Which to choose—day's descent
or this intermittent emptiness?

Black as the dark of the mouth's interior—
black as the tar of the far-gone stars.

Our interest lies in what might burn—
which last and lonely joy
of taste and lip and tongue.

I bend to your position
lie to lie
in all that ends.

He went wide of the landing and stumbled through the shore willows, whimpering and pushing with his thin arms at things in the night. Then he was standing alone on the shore.

Come to the edge in this soil called country, this dirt called grave.

Moon pulls our watered flesh ever further into night.

      We/Sediment   We/Clay

A roof not enough, a wall. Our history lies in the whim of water—
the elusive, ever-shifting contour of the shore.

Water licks the margin: women
wash and hold their hair:

the wombing and the waste,
borderland/ or overlord.

      Another atmosphere, its unsung lungs.

      Swallow and swallow, hemming the stone.

Calloused fingers hold your tongue—
body to the body of the land-bound song.

That night they were visited with a plague of hail out of a faultless sky and the horses shied and moaned and the men dismounted and sat upon the ground with their saddles over their heads while the hail leaped in the sand like small lucent eggs concocted alchemically out of the desert darkness.

Things fall.
Clouds, contrail,
passing birds that cast
no shadow.

I receive the animal
carved into relic
carved into ruin—
your hungers
exposed
into this
atmosphere,

an emptiness
our eyes once made
to hold the weight and heft
of so much longing.

What harvest of ruin
can you gather
in your mouth
once the threat
of storm is passing—

a void of hoar frost,
fog and brume
& this last windfall
translucency.

What's he a judge of? He said. What's he a judge of? What's he a judge of.

Candles make black
shadows dance
along the contours
of your skin.

You would have me
kneel through the streets—
tell the earth's uncaring
ear my least transgression.

Spun from the fronds of
spring, the inner workings
of a worm, budded there
robe-red as a womb,
gold-scented—you
would be this woman
faithful to the last because
believe, believe
in the eyes that count
your mercy
and your sin.

I have lost the stem
of this flower, I have
dropped the calm, cool
palm of the saint
who led me in.

The large ear holds my
evidence. I am nothing
but a bird, a seed,
a storm's recurrent slip of wind.

He's left behind the pinewood country and the evening sun declines before him beyond an endless swale and dark falls here like a thunderclap and a cold wind sets the weeds to gnashing.

It's curtains. Stage dark.
Exit left, my empathy.
The trees full of feathers.
The night full of gowns.

I am not a real thing;
just part of the migration.
I walked all day to
put you at my heels.
Now your teeth
have a taste for
every hunger.

You assume domesticity
but I am wilder
than this weather—
The fact of my ritual
no smaller than the sun
—going up
—coming down.

Wait for the sky to change
& see what I've known all along.
When the new thirst comes
you'll beg &
beg but find the water
gone.

The sun to the west lay in a holocaust where there rose a steady column of small desert bats and to the north along the trembling perimeter of the world dust was blowing down the void like the smoke of distant armies.

To this

  I add your face as it

Registers   dawn.

That I see you   that I am near.

That your pulse is the steadiness

by which I gauge the air.

This air, that blows   down the

void.

To the void   I add my hands, empty

as wings

spread

to catch
the plume

of night's last burning.

They cut the throats of the pack animals and jerked and divided the meat and they traveled under the cape of the wild mountains upon a broad soda plain with dry thunder to the south and rumors of light.

Cape of the mountains
cloak of time
worn, worn platitudes.

Beseech me
of the dry land,
bequeath me
one more day.

Without horizon
the sky's long loom
knits tattered shawls
to our eternities.

Thirst's last stanch
and this inevitable
new weather.

... and the horse was watching, out there past men's knowing, where the stars are drowning and whales ferry their vast souls through the black and seamless sea.

What the ocean wants
is everything—
I, too, need such salt
upon my tongue.

The waves lift
the waves descend—
a decorous measure
once the body leans
into the grave
of its own longings,
shrill as blue water,
infinite mirror.

Ocean, ocean.
eat the past
away like acid.
If this is the wash,
wash us
wholly down.

... the moonblanched waste lay before them cold and pale and the moon sat in a ring overhead and in that ring lay a mock moon with its own cold gray and nacre seas.

One metaphor inside another—
a cup in a cup in a cup and a ball.
Inside the bed an old woman
worried to thread by equally
old hands. Inside her clothes,
beast & tooth & fur.

The ground is built on shifts—
it heaves its great uncertainty
and after this, what then, what then.

The girl arrives, seduced
and swallowed by a lie.
Call the man with the knife,
slit out and out— the crone,
the girl—the squeamish mess.

What is real, what false,
sand or oyster, host or guest?
The moon a mere reflection
of the sun.

Inside the woman
more women—
inside of them
how many men?

You can find meanness in the least of creatures, but when God made man the devil was at his elbow. A creature that can do anything. Make a machine. And a machine to make the machine. An evil that can run itself a thousand years, no need to tend it.

Crude mechanisms with our mouths in the air, gasp and utter/utter gasp/inimitable red/inimitable egg, all tit and squelch/our nests full of fledglings lie dead/in their feathers.

Through our desolate splendor of be be be/oh turbine of mine soul/the flesh machine is a woman's hoodoo/Can dissect can devise, can peer and prod/ yet a thousand years and the instruments/ still reaching/Here that we are /that we are that /we are/ hinged together with wire and bone.

I put my lips to your chest and get a taste for flesh/ rich salt/the unguent phrases/I get a taste for writing in the clouds.

Make my arms out of tape and tin cans/my eyes from stones/make me something of belief because / my body is and wills/Stop the world from its mad/ mad blooming/even fire pops the cherries of the seeds.

Forget the satellite's click and wheeze/machine eternity/ is wired to a bomb/ Tick/ tick/ Tick tock/ The body is/ our otherwise/This nerve collapse// Mine   digits.

...and one whose horse's whole head was painted crimson red and all the horsemen's faces gaudy and grotesque with daubings like a company of mounted clowns, death hilarious, all howling in a barbarous tongue and riding down upon them like a horde from a hell more horrible yet than the brimstone land of Christian reckoning.

Hope's bleak horses
ride like hunger
into the decaying
vastness of our ever
crumbing architectures.

After
there is nothing
or more
of what
we'll never see.

His friends rode small and colorful horses that forty days ago had been wild animals on the plain and they shied and skittered and snapped like turtles.

Conjure oppositions;
they drive like mules.
Wild. Whiled.
Teeth and bone.
(A shrill trill of avid birds.)

The body is available,
(peck here, peck there)
& train each upstart
out of it.

Forty days to holy
or withheld. Distill
its iconography.
(Crow, vulture, crows.)

Your hands hold the tools
of a docile new religion—
what it takes
to break the animal—
a whip & a clock
and a man to ride
you steady.

The rifle carried a vernier sight on the tang and he would eye the distance and gauge the wind and set the sight like a man using a micrometer.

My father studied the last digits and first inchings, his own hands scripts and numerals. Ever the plumb line, ever the level; but the curved & flesh-made spill and spill. There are gains beyond the eye's firm margins not countable or known. Set a caliper to the iris of a whale, a compass to a maude of circling crows—all mystery beyond the crosshair's lone intention. To make prey of all the living we might own.

His folk are known for hewers of wood and drawers of water but in truth his father has been a schoolmaster. He lies in drink, he quotes from poets whose names are now lost. The boy crouches by the fire and watches him.

This loss language
lists its alphabet.

You'd have my tongue
but I've yours first—

a lick and a lick and a lilt.

Shadows
in the embers form an eye—

whereas your heart,
bitter weed—

beats & beats
rich anapests of salt and greed.

There is room on the stage for one beast and one alone. All others are destined for a night that is eternal and without name. One by one they will step down into the darkness before the footlamps. Bears that dance, bears that don't.

Recall
that milksweet
you-mouth
plenty oh plenty
drip & spill
all the humid summer
I liked to breathe
the apples in
liked to bite
you lightly
we could be mingled
in the world
shit in the shit
of foodlust
& story
the fruit
sweet beyond its
skin & also in its
maggotmouthed
undoing
come to my side
& lick my wounds
the rest have died
all died
then come, again
me too

The First Violence

This is a concrete/visual poem with text scattered across the page. Reading the fragments approximately by spatial position:

All night / was weather / I thought the sky,

The / I suckle / I took for hope / whose susurrus the moan
what / wind ever-blows
decay. / whose salt is not the body / and
everything
the brown
neglect
antic death's

whose / Eternity / a long, flat palm / feast or / This desert,
of your body

your windblown name
the skirmish

Burned / lisping in the sky / fest / our present / *the wind*
insists the sand / *Sand in*
, erodes the letters. / new suit. / black / Summer
into of
the moon
like

by the sun, a fateful / bleed days
of / eustacy
nameless sea / whose / the fine ash
new blades, and who
punish and what are

bleed out, while / of. / admit / examined food or feed. / Elsewhere,
has are we
to we to be?

wings signal / has / *blew and the fine dust set their teeth on edge,*
autumn— / *everything, grit in all they ate.*

the rock's red veins
at the withered spoon of once

what / land into the sea—
remnant of the body,

all we used to be.

```
                                                                              As the juggler
                                                                                             with strange posturings under the lapsing flare of the torches.
                                                    I can't say lip,
                                                    my eye
                                                    through lurid
                                                    --skin reading
                              my first illiteracy
                              without the lip
                                                                   into origin

                                                    death's        extrudes the
                                                                                  world
                                                                                  fenestrations.
                                    I can't                     without your name
                                    say lip,                    stench
                                                        turned without your name with a sweep of his without your name arm the girl gave him a shove and he
                                    this                your name from the tent and strode abo without your name ut
                                    tongue
                       I can't
                       say lip,
                                    skin--or
                                    nuance


               into origin

               extrudes the       this
                                  tongue


                                    skin--or
                                    nuance
    into origin

    extrudes the


                              my first illiteracy




                                                                     leaped without


turned with a sweep of his arm the girl gave him a shove and he leaped from the tent and strode about
```

Your heart's desire   *is to be*
                                                                                               told
                                          & cauterized the trees   *some*
Birds||No birds.   *mystery.*
too cold to flit   your hand//your   *The*
        among the   *mystery*
leaves   & cauterized the trees   *is that*
                                                                                               there is
                                                                                               no
an embalmed music-   *mystery.*
-   & cauterized the trees
Winter is a glass
                                          your hand//your
                                                     In the punctuation of silence
                                                     Or silence:
                                          & cauterized the trees
                           punctuated.
                           silence: everything in exterior
     Winter is a glass Winter

          world

                                                              it crystalized the running
                                                              sap
     punctuated. silence: Winter is a glass Winter is   All day you moved
                                                              these ever falling
                                                              trees
it crystalized the running sap
All day you moved
these ever falling
trees   fro
                                     Birds||No birds.   zen
                                     too cold to flit   like winter
                                             among the   flowers
                                     leaves

                                                                                 punctuated.
     silence: Winter is a glass   Winter prismatic
     silence: Winter is a glass   an embalmed music-   Winter
                                     -
                   hands   Winter is a glass   which hold

In the punctuation of silence
Or silence: Winter is a glass Winter is a glass

silence: Winter is a glass Winter

Burned
lisping in the sky
new suit.

by the sun, a fateful
eustacy was weather   I took for hope
whose   wind ever-blows
             I thought the sky,
                      whose salt is not the body
             whose susurrus the
                 moan
        your windblown name
              the skirmish

insists the sand   land into the sea—
, erodes the letters   and   remnant of the body,
                     everything
                     the brown
          bleed days   all we used to be.
                neglect
                     antic death's
of   the fine ash
nameless sea   new blades, and who
                     punish and what are

              Elsewhere,
              has are we
              to we to be?

used to be Summer and everything the moan of all we has burned into whose susurrus.the brown neglect of of the body autumn—the moon but the remnant lisping in the sky not the body like antic death's whose salt is new suit. This gritty, nameless sea desert, our present a the sea— the long, flat palm examined the land into by the sun, wind ever-blows, a fateful eustacy sky, decay. The whose black wings I thought the signal feast or was weather what fest food or took for hope feed.Eternity insists once what I the sand admit withered spoon of the fine ash while at the of your body, out, bleed days, erodes the letters red veins bleed of your windblown I suckle the rock's name. Elsewhere, the skirmish are we to be has new blades, punish and what? and who are we

used to be Summer and everything the moan of all we has burned into whose susurrus.the brown neglect of of the body autumn—the moon but the remnant lisping in the sky not the body like antic death's whose salt is new suit. This gritty, nameless sea desert, our present a the sea— the long, flat palm examined the land into by the sun, wind ever-blows, a fateful eustacy sky, decay. The whose black wings I thought the signal feast or was weather what fest food or took for hope feed.Eternity insists once what I the sand admit withered spoon of the fine ash while at the of your body, out, bleed days, erodes the letters red veins bleed of your windblown I suckle the rock's name. Elsewhere, the skirmish are we to be has new blades, punish and what? and who are we

used to be Summer and everything the moan of all we has burned into whose susurrus.the brown neglect of of the body autumn—the moon but the remnant lisping in the sky not the body like antic death's whose salt is new suit. This gritty, nameless sea desert, our present a the sea— the long, flat palm examined the land into by the sun, wind ever-blows, a fateful eustacy sky, decay. The whose black wings I thought the signal feast or was weather what fest food or took for hope feed.Eternity insists once what I the sand admit withered spoon of the fine ash while at the of your body, out, bleed days, erodes the letters red veins bleed of your windblown I suckle the rock's name. Elsewhere, the skirmish are we to be has new blades, punish and what? and who are we

used to be Summer and everything the moan of all we has burned into whose susurrus.the brown neglect of of the body autumn—the moon but the remnant lisping in the sky not the body like antic death's whose salt is new suit. This gritty, nameless sea desert, our present a the sea— the long, flat palm examined the land into by the sun, wind ever-blows, a fateful eustacy sky, decay. The whose black wings I thought the signal feast or was weather what fest food or took for hope feed.Eternity insists once what I the sand admit withered spoon of the fine ash while at the of your body, out, bleed days, erodes the letters red veins bleed of your windblown I suckle the rock's name. Elsewhere, the skirmish are we to be has new blades, punish and what? and who are we

used to be Summer and everything the moan of all we has burned into whose susurrus.the brown neglect of of the body autumn—the moon but the remnant lisping in the sky not the body like antic death's whose salt is new suit. This gritty, nameless sea desert, our present a the sea— the long, flat palm examined the land into by the sun, wind ever-blows, a fateful eustacy sky, decay. The whose black wings I thought the signal feast or was weather what fest food or took for hope feed.Eternity insists once what I the sand admit withered spoon of the fine ash while at the of your body, out, bleed days, erodes the letters red veins bleed of your windblown I suckle the rock's name. Elsewhere, the skirmish are we to be has new blades, punish and what? and who are we

used to be Summer and everything the moan of all we has burned into whose susurrus.the brown neglect of of the body autumn—the moon but the remnant lisping in the sky not the body like antic death's whose salt is new suit. This gritty, nameless sea desert, our present a the sea— the long, flat palm examined the land into by the sun, wind ever-blows, a fateful eustacy sky, decay. The whose black wings I thought the signal feast or was weather what fest food or took for hope feed.Eternity insists once what I the sand admit withered spoon of the fine ash while at the of your body, out, bleed days, erodes the letters red veins bleed of your windblown I suckle the rock's name. Elsewhere, the skirmish are we to be has new blades, punish and what? and who are we

used to be Summer and everything the moan of all we has burned into whose susurrus.the brown neglect of of the body autumn—the moon but the remnant lisping in the sky not the body like antic death's whose salt is new suit. This gritty, nameless sea desert, our present a the sea— the long, flat palm examined the land into by the sun, wind ever-blows, a fateful eustacy sky, decay. The whose black wings I thought the signal feast or was weather what fest food or took for hope feed.Eternity insists once what I the sand admit withered spoon of the fine ash while at the of your body, out, bleed days, erodes the letters red veins bleed of your windblown I suckle the rock's name. Elsewhere, the skirmish are we to be has new blades, punish and what? and who are we

used to be Summer and everything the moan of all we has burned into whose susurrus.the brown neglect of of the body autumn—the moon but the remnant lisping in the sky not the body like antic death's whose salt is new suit. This gritty, nameless sea desert, our present a the sea— the long, flat palm examined the land into by the sun, wind ever-blows, a fateful eustacy sky, decay. The whose black wings I thought the signal feast or was weather what fest food or took for hope feed.Eternity insists once what I the sand admit withered spoon of the fine ash while at the of your body, out, bleed days, erodes the letters red veins bleed of your windblown I suckle the rock's name. Elsewhere, the skirmish are we to be has new blades, punish and what? and who are we

used to be Summer and everything the moan of all we has burned into whose susurrus.the brown neglect of of the body autumn—the moon but the remnant lisping in the sky not the body like antic death's whose salt is new suit. This gritty, nameless sea desert, our present a the sea— the long, flat palm examined the land into by the sun, wind ever-blows, a fateful eustacy sky, decay. The whose black wings I thought the signal feast or was weather what fest food or took for hope feed.Eternity insists once what I the sand admit withered spoon of the fine ash while at the of your body, out, bleed days, erodes the letters red veins bleed of your windblown I suckle the rock's name. Elsewhere, the skirmish are we to be has new blades, punish and what? and who are we

used to be Summer and everything the moan of all we has burned into whose susurrus.the brown neglect of of the body autumn—the moon but the remnant lisping in the sky not the body like antic death's whose salt is new suit. This gritty, nameless sea desert, our present a the sea— the long, flat palm examined the land into by the sun, wind ever-blows, a fateful eustacy sky, decay. The whose black wings I thought the signal feast or was weather what fest food or took for hope feed.Eternity insists once what I the sand admit withered spoon of the fine ash while at the of your body, out, bleed days, erodes the letters red veins bleed of your windblown I suckle the rock's name. Elsewhere, the skirmish are we to be has new blades, punish and what? and who are we

The Meridians

Yes the wind blows down the yellow sky like the last breath of an ailing god yes I breathe it yes I run yes the sky maws anew yes each dangerous new appellation of doom's dormant wiring. yes I have lost my agency yes my will. yes if you asked me. yes I would say. this too. this too is beauty.

What if I went out what if I crossed it what if on dead horse what if remembered what if the weapon what if my thumb what if the ending what if you made me what if I wasn't what of I am what if was taken what if the full moon what if the tea leaves what if the chalk what if I willed it what if i knew what of the basalt what of the shrew what of what if what if I too?

Ghost Lyrics 2

He began to speak with a strange urgency of things.

I go out and never in, mind adrift—
embankments of white
like feathers ripped from breasts,
like beds inside beds—

my hands gnarled as old machines.
Last night the owl 'twas low and moaned,
filled the space of my restiveness with
death's black margin.

My lips stutter
into clunks and mutters.
Say, say, the will to say.
Around this day, all the days
strewn about like dirty clothes.

Somewhere,
a thousand birds
deny their constancy
and leave this season
for another.

Somewhere, our intentions.
And somewhere
everything—
just think of it all.

It's a notion, no more. But someplace in the scheme of things this world must touch the other.

Give me your ghost lips and your dew-soaked garments. Whisper all the past alive where you sat your days in one small chair, there by the stove amid the grease of lamb asoot with combustion in your eyes seeing elsewhere, bare rooms and rosaries, the seam of things snip snip/snip snip. You fell to the kindness of a long-haired prophet but he's tied behind the altar where the bishops bleached your mouth. Never is your knowing, always after or before. Tuck inside some cell your keening eye— that bluest bird. So much dissolution that the future must come down to consecrate the past. The line between us fingertip, mine to yours; yours to mine.

I take it ye lost your way, said the hermit.

Out this ever-many road,
bare-toed to my condition,
I ate a portion of my shoes.
No magnet in the earth
could pull me near
—the time I knew of nothing,
nothing still.

Whistle my name into
some southern ballad,
lash a something
round my knee.
I've wormed full west
but come no closer
to the sea.

Say of wasp, say of woman,
hoarde-fat or empty of—
say never and you shear
away her name.
Not respite, not shelter—
roads away
and more roads.

I drive days like mules
across the dark's regression
Up, west or east—
my feet a paltry slap
against the asphalt's
flat aggressions.

A warm wind was blowing and the east held a gray light. The fowls roosting among the grapevines had begun to stir and call.

I came up from beneath
like worms who know the ash
they taste is sweetest in the spring.

I came to taste lightening
in the fire-blasted trees
lick the crocus heads alive—
sweet skeletons of bees.

Now, days.
More days.
Sun somewhere.
Stars somewhere else.

Distance/darkness
wait and call.

I came up from beneath
sugar-lipped
to chew & crawl.

The man who believes that the secrets of the world are forever hidden lives in mystery and fear.

I will tell you about the birds—
the hunting birds
and the nut birds
the birds who leave
and those who stay.

And here is the silver bird—
mercury in air—
and the red bird who comes
only in winter when the snow
makes of it a wound
and a holiness.

It makes no difference if you know
their names; they do not
know them either.

Call them the birds of discernment
and the birds of sorrow
the birds of blackest malice
or brightest beckoning.

Their bones are hollow—
their blood is cold.

They require emptiness
to place themselves—
cannot discern clear
glass from sky.

Without them
there is silence
and nowhere
to impale your desires,
but the songs they sing
lodge in your ears
like tiny sharpened
knives.

Grass and prickly pear grew on the roofs and goats walked about on them and somewhere off in that squalid kingdom of mud the sound of the little deathbells tolled thinly.

Berry mouth/mouth of spring.

The animals—alive—they
 stumble from their stupor.

Sweet onion of the air
—trillium and wolfbane.

The trees burst with their hunger.

What cold we became
lost to frost's full burial.

Now upspring/now bloom
honeysuckle spikenard
sweet sap, sweet suckle, sweet suck.

Put me in your mouth
that we might
starve again.

Words are things The words he is in possession of he cannot be deprived of. Their authority transcends his ignorance of their meaning.

A thing becomes thingish
as you name it—
and in the thing
another nothing.

Thing word. Thing world.
Thing of the thing a string.
Ravel/un/Revel

And this dirt. We route
through. Whisper.

The dust of everything—

macerated stars

that starved & fell & make

this thingly-maddened world.

The way of the transgressor is hard. God made this world, but he didn't make it to suit everbody, did he?

One winter my blood doubled—

one spring I came apart.

> (Ask the first
> about the last and the last what's first—
> ask one for two.)

You put the flat world on a plate and lapped it up.

> (Ask what it means to be
> this breast,
> this lip, this question.)

When you turned to me,
eyes black and endless—

> (Ask the doll
> about tranquility,
> a symbol for its meaning.)

I held off that infection—
put your hungry gaze away.

> (Ask the wounded
>   how they hobble—
>
> ask the women why
> they pray.)

She looked harried and she smiled at them and she had smuggled them sweets under her shawl and there were pieces of meat in the bottom of the bowls that had come from her own table.

Bent

        bentover

                bentov

                        erben

                                toverben

                                        dsbeen

                                                overbent

Over stove & over crib & over garden & over sick & over bed & over body

        &

undermen & fronted altars

                            Be[nt](o) v_er

        is & is

station/ovum

what's left what l[eft]over

& was
& now

is

Bent
Bent over

He made his way down through the trees and stood looking at the cold swirling waters. Then he waded out into the river like some wholly wretched baptismal candidate.

Fill your hands with the river

      (mouth) with the sea.

Do you dirty> do you> slick—

    do you slide the bottom-silt>old as a carp> and nattered?

Belly the shoal-dark<>belly the weeds—

pursuit

  hovers

in apostrophe.   Shadow strike   or damselfly.

Water, an atmosphere/water now impure

  —your life as scaled armor

  —your lips hung with their lures.

They pass a watercart in the street and they pass a hole in the wall where by the light of a small forgefire an old man beats out shapes of metal. They pass in a doorway a young girl whose beauty becomes the flowers about.

Grown round and round—

a pear and plum—

                                    perfumed to the nose

                                                fertile petal.

All that's missing

is your tongue.

But who builds in stone seeks to alter the structure of the universe and so it was with these masons however primitive their works may seem to us.

Red stones, old/old as oranges & onions, flowers & knives/grease to glim the engines/when whir-slap of looms when trolley hum/when we was a going enterprise/ yet the truth/ the truth lies in the scars/ in eternities spun from empty mouths & boots blown bottomout/how determined we trudged yet every hill another/now ruins protrude this valley/each murmur a dirge, each brick cenotaph/grind the organ/ clank the chains/you made me here as I made you/ahowl in the chinks, this timeblown masonry /each history shrieks necessity/each mother shreds her fable.

...and they rode through stands of sunflowers tall as a man on horseback, the dead faces dished toward the west. The country began to open up and they began to come upon plantings of corn on the hillsides and a few clearings in the wilderness where there were grass huts and orange and tamarind trees. Of humans they saw none.

Black night—
Black day—

pastures turned
with shit & fishscales
lush fecund unstirring.

The sheds
shed of rope and blade
of loopholes in the twine
leather smack on horseback
so owned so...
heads of the town look
up/ look down/ heads of the town—
what decorates the trees?

Come the gun
so the gun
corpses of the corn husks hung
in their beginnings.

Oh rich desolation
which grows and grows

they have killed all the fertile animals.

An old woman in a gray shawl was cutting up beef ribs with an axe while two dogs sat watching. A tall thin man in a blood-stained apron entered the room and looked them over. He leaned and placed both hands on the table before them.

The world grows better
reflected in death's eyes—

I want it everywhere on me,
a lick and lick and a tease—
death crooning with my tongue,
death spooning out its cream.

You whisper it was all for naught
but naught is all I own,
naught of infinite and ovary—
of the swallow, of the cum.

Death
I am the whole of you.
Flesh and raunch and smell.
Exquisite energy—
a dot of never—
and this fine, collapsing sun.

He sees a parricide hanged in a crossroads hamlet and the man's friends run forward and pull his legs and he hangs dead from his rope while urine darkens his trousers.

To kill the father is a crime.
Dance, they said,
but he preferred
to pray.

How little we know of ourselves
until the animal convenes.
We could cast our vagaries
in shawls of silk, build shrines
from stolen teeth.

And yet, thirst compels
the stuttered tongue
and so it started all again,
washing the water
with the water.

When she arrived,
her hands felt the evident
loss of invocation—wasted
flesh that dangled from a need.

They wrapped their hands
in ropes of hair,
licked the rank salt
from his body.

They did this that they might begin anew
and bring the body to the body once again
like a woman might possess herself—
each hollow full of other,
the taste of a man
dying slowly in her mouth.

Have mercy on me. Todos Muertos. Todos.

What do we owe the dead
aside from living—our names
etched in the paper remnants
of their skin like a map of the future.

Here, it diagrams oblivion—
snowfields of nothing
in this temporary winter,
in this rich, eternal spin.

I wish to capture something
in my palm and keep it—
a ghost of light, the shape
of shadow as it moves through
distortion—you, among the
trees, your face whiter
for the blackness of sky,
like a tundra swan
curving the bend of land
around its body.

To be is to be blinded
in a white-wash of signals,
discerning the edge
of this opaque,
imagined world.

Three men sat on the box not unlike the dead themselves or spirit folk so white they were with lime and nearly phosphorescent in the dusk. A pair of horses drew the cart and they went up the road in a faint miasma of carbolic and passed from sight.

Up-go ghosts/up-go and walk/
the moon glues all your shadows to the trees/

Up-go again/and stir the vats of was/
and walk the stairs/ and screech the walls/

Your skin white as chalk/
luminous as pinworms /

Come to me/ in the middle space of sleep
when I am lonely in my longing/just to know

Stumble in on your centuries/your wooden shoes/
I lie here in the density of living/ now full-blown

Come take me to the cloudiness/
of once/ the vapor of again/

This husk wars with me/ presses
years upon my skin/

Up-go ghosts/
I was nothing once/ will be that then again.

The Second Violence

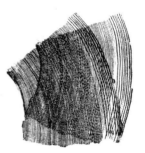

They cut the throats of the pack animals and jerked and divided the meat and they traveled under the cape of the wild mountains upon a broad soda plain with dry thunder to the south and rumors of light.

Cape of the mountains
Cloak of the day
Worn worn platitudes

Beseech me
Of the dry land, bequeath me
One more day

without
Horizon
the sky's long
loom
knits tattered shawls
to our eternities

thirst's stanch
and this inevitable
new weather

He went wide of the landing and stumbled through the shore
Water licks the margin: women
wash and hold their

.

Come to the edge in this soil called   country, this
dirt called grave.

                A roof Another atmosphere, its unsung lungs.
we/sediment   enough, a   we/

clay

wall. Our history lies in the whim of water
                        The elusive, ever-shifting contour of the shore.

                        Water licks the margin: women
                        wash and hold their hair:
                                              the wombing and the waste,
                    Swallow and swallow, hemming the stone   borderland/ or overlord.
                      Another atmosphere, its unsung lungs.

                                          Flailing fingers,

body to the body   Moon pulls our watered flesh ever further into night.
of the land-bound
song.

and one whose horse's whole head was painted crimson red and all the horsemen's faces gaudy and grotesque with daubings like a company of mounted clowns, death hilarious, all howling in a barbarous tongue and riding down upon them like a horde from a hell more horrible yet than the brimstone land of Christian reckoning

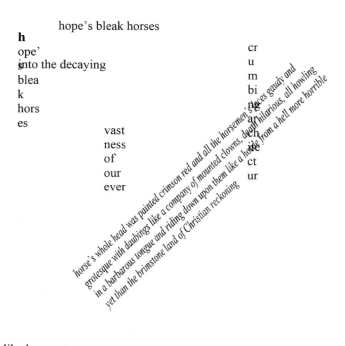

ride like hunger
into the decaying
vastness of our ever
crumbing architectures

after there is nothing
or more
of what we'll never see

                                            ride like hunger

God how the stars did fall. I looked for blackness, holes in the heavens. The Dipper stove.

```
                    you        Clear nights
        b   r   trained   u   g   h   t
        t   h   d a e         s   k   y       the earth's confusion—
        t   o   sharp
        y   o   lens  u   r
        e   y   beyond      —                 Left our gravity system
        y   o   d     u     r                 for an
        b   r   o     k  e  n
        e   y   e                             nevoid skin
```

                                                    show me the planets bloom like
                                                    even screen the sun that I might
                                                    understands the
                                                    earth the stars

moon

<small>Left our gravity system
for an alien else
Jupiter's nevoid skin
Milkrock</small>   I asked: I ask:
                        show me the planets

the sun that I might

our faces trained to the
night sky trying hard
to see past our impairments

```
                                b   r   o   u   g   h   t
                                t   h   e       s   k   y
                                t   o
                                    o   u   r
                                    y   e   —
                                    o   u   r
                                    b   r   o   k   e   n
                                    y   e
```

[rotated/inverted text elements repeating phrases: "our faces trained to the night sky trying hard to see past our impairments", "even screen the sun that I might", "show me the planets bloom like", "peonies", "I asked: I ask:", "show me the planets bloom like", and inverted "show me the planets", "even the earth at night", "understands the", "earth the stars"]

<small>Left our gravity system
for an alien else
Jupiter's nevoid skin
Milkrock</small>

63

Ghost Lyrics 3

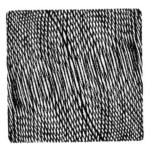

Whether in my book or not, every man is tabernacle in every other and he in exchange and so on in an endless complexity of being and witness to the uttermost edge of the world.

I have gone deep in
above my bobbing head

—in the middle place
between fish and lung.

Hypnotic light
tenebrious water

& the silence.

This is how you nest in me.

Silt-soft & half alive.

**

I find you bottomsung
—your hair streaming
milfoil, face Ophelia-white.
When I reach you
you whisper inflected phrases
I will never understand.

**

I find I cannot move—
that the trees are made a bier
upon the shore,
that the sky is
not an atmosphere
but a film
through which
your voice oscillates.
I feel the insistence
of your eyes
from the inside
of my body
which is gone
somehow, just
gone.

**

Once we drank
strong tea and talked
of empires.
I collected bits of you
in a box with rocks
and bird bones.
Now look at us—
stuck in the after-all
like a philosophical
problem.

**

I lived a long time
before the hatch
began, before
some latent urge
hooked my lip.
There is nothing
like a body
comes itself
inside you
kicking free.
Nothing so
profound
nor murky as
these waters.

**

Now in the dark
I strain to read
the paper floating
thinly in your hands.
Must be a code,
I think—
a code that tells me
who I need to be.
And yet
And yet

I cannot find your eyes
so cannot see.

**

I have gone deep —

The air is   absent—

What I float in—

or I am—

The huge carved and paneled doors hung awap on their hinges and a carved stone Virgin held in her arms a headless child.

a door is but a margin
my life a claim you made/made on me

margin entry
made of you

hold back/hold in
likenesses or statuary

one air/ two
I swim in all your will/not that I knew/ this mingling

you there, me here
          baptized in this/ / not/my/ /atmosphere

open wide and claim it
/dry winds/and sediment/

or lock against the past
/ these bodies/

our/ long
// abeyant//sea

He walked all night and still he could see the fires behind him.

This is a treatise on the past.

When I opened the window
no birds flew in,
yet the properties
of glass remained
a tunnel to the sky.

Life is a series of exiles
First, the body.
Last, the body.
The dress lost
its pleating.
The dog ran away.

Yet the sun was
a maddening orange. It said,
Come to the night
with a patch on your eye.
Come to the sea
with a hand-sewn sail.

The dog returned
with bleeding paws
trailing the scent
of what it had known—
old boxes, paper ruins.

Time remained—
remains—
directional
and linnets eat the flax
from which the linen's made.

I think she means to say that in your fortune lie our fortunes all.

A woman holds her palm
to sky, a feast
of ovaries upon it
plucked from
thorny bushes.

Birds map berries
to beaks &
augur in her palm
of juice & sweat
a human problem.

Futility
to reach the wild
through the known.

The future's
only certainty—
one is eaten
& one eats.

But where does a man come by his notions. What world's he seen that he liked better?

Cliff ridge above
ice-bound river—
snow just fallen
makes brides
of all the trees.

Below, a buck
splayed full broken,
a comb of gold
entombed in ice,
his antlered caul
tipped as though
to contemplate
the clouds.

Imagine his last
turn and wheel
—an astonishment
of birds.

And you above,
your lungs in your mouth
absorb the artistry
in each wrong angle,
the audacity of earth
to trip us
in our longings.

The wrath of God lies sleeping. It was hid a million years before men were and only men have power to wake it. Hell aint half full. Hear me. Ye carry war of a madman's making onto a foreign land. Ye'll wake more than the dogs.

Maps on the table,
maps in their mouths
the dirt drinks
all their violence.

They sniff of it.
mark their scent,
nitrous strong
& manganese
—make a province
of lamina, a nation-state
of womb.

Always you must rid the land
of the living, yet children
burr and cling.
Boots at the borders
belts at the wall
—their teeth set
on discovery.
Clear the women,
kill them first
and kill them well,

and when the blood
drains of death
and runs downhill
toward water—
the iron
the iron
how it fortifies
the soil.

Don't leave it out yonder somethin'll eat it. This is a hungry country.

>When you guide the rope along the flank go steady & go slow. No rush into its blood of fear's last residue lest we taste in the flesh some new distress and catch our teeth on the toughness of muscle. When you eat the sinew, gnaw the bone, when the fire dims and stars strike through the million-pinholed sky, arm against the shadow, back against the night. Good of your rope. Good of your gloves. A company of metal, the firm lap of your gun.

Your heart's desire is to be told some mystery. The mystery is that there is no mystery.

Winter is a glass world glinting
it crystalized the running sap
& cauterized the trees.

All day   you moved
in the punctuation of silence
or silence: punctuated.

Birds‖No birds.
Too cold to flit
among the leaves.

Everything in exterior
prismatic—
an embalmed music—
your hand//your hands
which hold

these ever-falling
trees.

As the juggler turned with a sweep of his arm the girl gave him a shove and he leaped from the tent and strode about with strange posturings under the lapsing flare of the torches.

This tongue
my eye
extrudes the world
through lurid fenestrations.

—skin reading
skin—or nuance
into origin.

Without the lip
I can't say lip—
without your name,
death's stench
my first illiteracy.

God how the stars did fall. I looked for blackness, holes in the heavens. The Dipper stove.

Clear nights you brought the sky
to your eye—your broken eye,
left our gravity system
for an alien else—
Jupiter's nevoid skin,
milkrock of moon.

One orbit out, you left
our starved atmosphere
weightless, new.

I asked: show me the planets
bloom like peonies—
even screen the sun
that I might understand
its smolder. Return
to these eternities where
the stars just go & go,

our faces trained
to the night sky
trying hard see beyond
the Earth's confusion.

Females of domestic reputation lounged upon the balconies they passed with faces gotten up in indigo and almagre gaudy as the rumps of apes and they peered from behind their fans with a kind of lurid coyness like transvestites in a madhouse.

You could put mirror in your eyes. And call. The world in. You could. Button a damselfly. Into noon bread. You could email options. You could. Bury the weeds. You could. Feel it then. Fluid. Decay. You could. Bend the piano. You. Could. Pepper the tea. You. Could feed them. Your body. You could. Door through the keys. You could darken. The whites. You. Could. Dust the debris. You could rip. All the linens. Corset the dogs. You could. Toast to the wretched. Enamor. The hogs. You could cuckle. The chickens you. Could bash them. With sticks you. Could drive through. The garden. You could sell. All your tricks. You could open. Your vulva and enter. The store. You could mime. On the sidewalk. Fall on. The pure. You could e-bill. The i-man for ooing your ahhs. You. Could ass. Or astonish. Or butt and betray. You could sex. In the minefield. You. Could weekend. Away. You could nuclear option. Abort or condone. You could. Vote. With. Your ovary. Could. Engage. It with drones. You could aspic. McDonalds. You could $3.99. You. Could fluff. All the lampshades. You. Could braid. All. The lines. You could straighten. That curl you. Could handle. Those drugs. You. Could vaginal. Dryness one day. At a time you. Could lean in or. Lean out. You could fuck. This alone. You could work. For the same you. Could same for. The work. You could fist it. Could kneel. Could. Moan or cajole. You could lipstick. Ecstatic. Use. All your clout. You could pluck it. Or hotwax. Could simper. Could pout. Put mirrors. In. Your eyes and. Then. Turn inside. Out.

The gifts of the Almighty are weighed and parceled out in a scale peculiar to himself. It's no fair accountin and I dont doubt but what he'd be the first to admit it and you put the query to him boldface.

Death and its daubings
its cocktails
first, life later—
nights of were
and would
between my legs.

It all goes carnival,
cold
as your
mouth
and red,

the game rigged
and the end
all we ever
walk away with.

This Final Margin

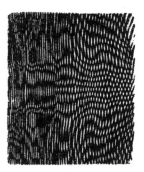

Dream. I am walking down a dark and narrow corridor with many doors, like an inn or institution. My job: to open each and gain entry. My grandmother and I watched game shows together because of our sickness for hope and this is just like *Let's Make a Deal.* Choose a door and get whatever lies behind it, a luxury vacation or a tragic pair of socks. Same orphan grandmother whose brothers raised her to dubious adulthood and who knows what in the interim. Behind door number one, she is chain-smoking, eyes on the middle distance, holding back, holding in.

I knock softly on the next door. No one stirs. Grab
the knob and twist, slowly push it in. Sheer and utter
darkness; a darkness so dark it is has solidity. There is no
way to enter this viscous atmosphere. I reach my arms
in front of me, but they get stuck, tarred in black and
sticky pitch. A heartbeat pulses through the air, softly.
A feeling of deep comfort—and deeper, some despair.

Behind this door, a nursery, painted bright yellow, fireplace crackling, beautiful wooden toys, dolls and their small furnishings. On the floor, a live rabbit in a wooden cradle, wearing glasses reads a book. Two ravens at a table drinking tea. I sit cross-legged on the floor and help myself to a plate of cookies. The ravens clear their throats. One cocks its head and looks at me reproachfully. A clock ticks in the background. The rabbit holds a book of fairy tales and begins to read us the story of the *Snow Queen*. I fall asleep, then wake alone with bird nests in my hair.

The fourth door is hot to the touch, screams, high-pitched and animal. I knock loudly, yell—wrench the knob, but it won't turn. Over and over, the screams persist. Flames crackling, acrid smoke beneath the sill. Finally, I force my shoulder to the door to find the room blackened into ash—ash ash, heaped in sculptural mounds, Lot's wife turned not to crystalline white salt, but the black dust of the devil's making.

I knock three times and the door flies open. Inside, a vast room filled with ornate mirrors, like Versailles. In the center a huge wing-backed chair faces away from me, the only furnishing. I walk nervously watching endless reflections of myself in the multitudes of mirror, but in each I am slightly different. A different dress, different hair. When I arrive behind the chair—the same chair that in the mirror across from me sits empty—someone speaks sardonically; a voice I know, but can't pin down. *Have you come to inquire of the truth?* Then a body in the chair stands up. The body is the outline of a woman whose flesh is liquid mirror. I see myself distorted in its mercury surface whose margins shift and grow, shrink, diminish, disappear. I move my head to see if its head also moves but it does not. Then laughter strikes a shadow through the room. I know that I should turn and run, but the mirror arm reaches out and suddenly, the I, the room—everything is gone.

A heavy door, mahogany, or maybe lead painted to look like mahogany. When I finally heave it open after much pulling and exertion, another door appears. I open that, and another, and so on and so on. *I think, One more. One more and then I'll stop,* but a compulsion has gripped me and I cannot; I must go on.

I creep down the hall to the last door on the left, much smaller than the others, painted robin's egg blue. I knock and a muffled voice calls, *In, in, in!* The room is Victorian—fern-patterned wallpaper, a huge four-poster bed, but there are no walls on the side of the room facing me, and the trees have become part of the interior, huge leafy limbs everywhere. A figure crouches in the branches, small and dark-haired. She says, *So flitting birds come straightway in,* and I know it's Emily Dickinson. I ask if she needs help getting down. She says, *This nest is ample eiderdown.* The air has an electric charge as though prophesizing storms. A rustle, a flap of wings and she is gone.

Behind this door, a card table and seated around it, all the women in my family, every last one, but here they are all the same age, somewhere in their twenties, and they're all wearing simple grey flannel dresses, their hair pulled into severe, tight buns. They've been drinking—bottles litter the room, and they're laughing like lunatics. I ask them what's so funny but they can't hear me, can't see me. They're laughing so hard they cannot breathe.

This door admits me to a hospital room, an old-fashioned one—a ward with roughly fifty beds—huge windows, metal dressers on wheels. Each bed contains a woman, each wildly different from the next—a mix of races, ethnicities, sizes, ages. A sea of difference, and yet, each has had the same message embroidered into her lips, which has sewn her mouth closed in the making. They stare wide-eyed at the ceiling and do not stir as I walk around and try to read. Neatly stitched into their skin is a cursive rendering of the phrase "role model.' Their eyes are unfocused as though they've been drugged. A doctor arrives in a white lab coat holding bandages and scalpels. He is tall, oily haired, black eyes flashing with derision. He says, *Oh good—a new one. I've been making such progress.* I ask if he's been hired by the government, but he sneers and claims to be a free agent, an artist, a leader of men. I wake with my fists clenched so tightly, my nails have drawn blood.

When I open this door, I'm in a cave, dimly lit by torches fastened to the walls, and shining through the torchlight, paintings of incredible color and shape—abstract paintings, but faces and bodies working through. A kind of delicate graffiti art, and in the flickering shadow, they seem to come alive, the walls shifting and moving like the hide of an animal. It is an animal—an elephant tied up in the darkness. It turns its head to look at me, her body ghoulish and wonderful, then stretches her trunk toward me, which disturbs me, the trunk like a separate creature, cartoonish but unsettling. The trunk works its way up my leg and around my neck, feeling along my jaw. I look into the elephant's eyes to discern her intention, and for all the world, she is laughing at me. She winds her trunk into my hair, mussing it up, patting my head.

Nearly at the end of the hall, a black door. Inside, a small theater, the entire place empty, a red curtain drawn across the stage. I sit, and instantly the lights go down and the curtains whoosh open. The judge sits naked, fat, and bald on a stool center stage, the spotlight on him, the remainder of the room in utter darkness. He begins to sing *My Funny Valentine* in a high falsetto. In his hand he holds a single rose that he periodically puts to his nose, caresses. Mid-song, he stops, stands. Holds out his hand. From stage right, a version of myself appears, naked, weeping. I/she, approaches, head in hands—in full despair, the judge now grinning ear to ear. He says, *Sing, darling! Sing!* I/she gets on her knees, supplicant, begging him, no, no. He grabs our hair, pulls our face closer to his own, and spits through clenched teeth, *Sing.* Half crying, half singing, we stutter through the first verse of *Somewhere Over the Rainbow,* which sends him into peals of high-pitched laughter. He pulls us to our feet and begins to pluck out all the petals of the rose, with each intoning in a theatrical baritone, *She loves me, she loves me not.* The last petal falls on *She loves me not.* He shakes his head sadly, sympathetically. *Well, flower.... you love me not. Tsk tsk tsk.* The I/she onstage begins to protest, but he pulls out of thin air a hunting knife and as he laughs, louder and louder, the curtain falls. I am colder, suddenly, than I have ever been before.

When I open this door, I'm in my grandmother's front yard, grasshoppers mad among the cosmos, my mother and grandmother sitting on the porch, smoking silently. When I approach, they glare at me and begin to softly chant, *You never knew!* Chanting louder and louder in unison, banging their fists on the old grey wooden porch floor, chanting and stomping at full volume. I wave my arms to try and make them stop. *Knew what? Tell me! Tell me!* They both stand and unbutton their shirts, their breasts and chests, upper arms marked with a cross-hatching of angry scars, words and numerals, lines and geometric forms. From my vantage, they look like maps, but the lines pulse and move. They're both furious, but suddenly mute. I can't tell exactly what they want me to see. My mother finds her voice and points to her chest. There's a curious scarring there, circular but indistinct. She whispers, eyes wild, *Emptied! Carved out by degrees.*

There is one door left. I turn the handle and hesitantly peer in. I'm in a library of Borges' imagination, rich wooden shelves lined floor to ceiling with books. As I enter, each aisle stretches in seemingly infinite arcs and curves, and the further into the library I get, it is less a building than a landscape. Bookshelves run along streams, through gardens, become in places, moss-covered. Deer nibble the corners of the older paperbacks, snails seek the binding glue. It is fantastically silent, running water and birdcall the only sounds that punctuate the quiet. People can be found burrowed in every corner reading. It takes me some time to realize there are only women here, though they're strangely ephemeral—not quite real. And that each time a book is opened, a new one appears.

I don't know what I am but I am not this body only;
every woman a distance from her skin by some measure
of the measure of the world. I stand behind a door of
self that is only part a form and peer out, watchful of
movements, wary of the men. As in this telling, women
lurk in thresholds, part captive, part threat. Wait for the
ire to eat up all the air. Then return to blow the smolder
of a ruined world into fire.

About the Author
Marci Nelligan is the author of *Infinite Variations* (Black Radish, 2011) and numerous chapbooks, and co-editor of *Intersections,* an interdisciplinary book on Jane Jacobs. Her work has appeared or is forthcoming in *Boog City, Jacket, the Denver Quarterly, The New Orleans Review, How2, Fledgling Rag,* and other journals. She teaches creative writing at Franklin & Marshall College.

About the Artist
Anthony Ryan received his BFA in printmaking in 1991 from Purchase College, State University of New York and his MFA in printmaking in 2008 from San Francisco State University. Selected recent exhibitions include *Playforms,* Woodland Gallery Chatham University, Pittsburgh, Pennsylvania (2013); *Centering the Margin,* Root Division, San Francisco, CA (2012); *One Thing Leads to Another: Seriality in Works on Paper,* San Jose Institute of Contemporary Art (2012); *Metrics* with Dana Hemenway, Park Life Gallery, San Francisco (2011); *Vision of New Fields* Project Space, Headlands Center for the Arts, Sausalito, CA (2010); and *New Prints 2009/Spring,* International Print Center New York (2009).